Date: 11/26/18

Grizzly Bears

By H.W. Poole

Children's Press®
An Imprint of Scholastic Inc.

Content Consultant
Nikki Smith
Assistant Curator, North America and Polar Frontier
Columbus Zoo and Aquarium

Library of Congress Cataloging-in-Publication Data

Names: Poole, Hilary W., author.
Title: Grizzly bears/by H.W. Poole.
Description: New York, NY: Children's Press, an imprint of Scholastic Inc., 2019. | Series: Nature's children |
Includes bibliographical references and index.
Identifiers: LCCN 2018002687| ISBN 9780531192627 (library binding) |
ISBN 9780531137550 (paperback)
Subjects: LCSH: Grizzly bear—Juvenile literature.
Classification: LCC QL737.C27 P6446 2019 | DDC 599.784—dc23
LC record available at https://lccn.loc.gov/2018002687

Design by Anna Tunick Tabachnik

Creative Direction: Judith E. Christ for Scholastic

Produced by Spooky Cheetah Press

Printed in North Mankato, MN, USA 113

SCHOLASTIC, CHILDREN'S PRESS, NATURE'S CHILDREN™, and associated logos
are trademarks and/or registered trademarks of Scholastic Inc.

1 2 3 4 5 6 7 8 9 10 R 28 27 26 25 24 23 22 21 20 19

Scholastic Inc., 557 Broadway, New York, NY 10012.

Photos ©: cover: Steve Hinch Photography; 1: James Hager/Robert Harding Picture Library; 4 leaf silo and throughout:
stockgraphicdesigns.com; 4 top: Jim McMahon/Mapman ®; 5 child silo: All-Silhouettes.com; 5 bear silo and throughout:
oorka/Shutterstock; 5 bottom: Mark Raycroft/Minden Pictures; 7: Scott E Read/Shutterstock; 8: Ron Sanford/Science Source;
11: John Delapp/Design Pics/Getty Images; 13: Pete Ryan/Getty Images; 14: Naphat Photography/Getty Images; 17: Mc Donald
Wildlife Photog./Animals Animals; 18: Ronan Donovan/Getty Images; 21 top left: Whitney Cranshaw/Colorado State University/
Bugwood.org/Wikimedia; 21 top right: Laura Romin & Larry Dalton/Alamy Images; 21 bottom left: Drew Rush/Getty Images;
21 bottom right: Jordana Meilleur/Alamy Images; 22: Paul Sawer/Minden Pictures; 25: McPHOTO/picture alliance/
blickwinkel/M/Newscom; 27: MyLoupe/Getty Images; 28: Leonard Lee Rue III/Getty Images; 31: Ron Niebrugge/Alamy Images;
33: Field Museum Library/Getty Images; 34: Matthias Breiter/Minden Pictures; 37: Florilegius/Alamy Images; 38: Yva Momatiuk
and John Eastcott/Minden Pictures; 41: George McCarthy/Minden Pictures; 42 bottom left: Andy Rouse/Nature Picture Library;
42 top right: Sonsedska Yuliia/Shutterstock; 42 top left: GlobalP/iStockphoto; 43 bottom: taden/iStockphoto; 43 top right:
Iakov Filimonov/Shutterstock; 43 top left: John Delapp/Design Pics/Getty Images.

Table of Contents

Fact File: Grizzly Bears

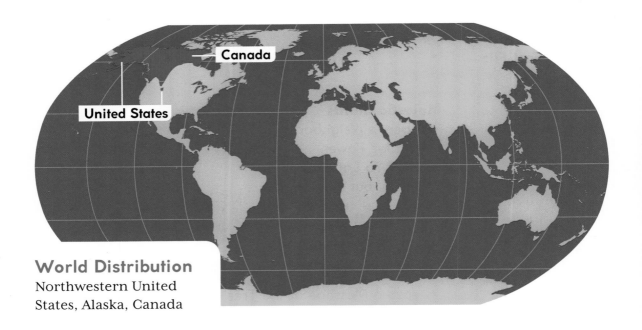

Canada

United States

World Distribution
Northwestern United States, Alaska, Canada

Habitat
Mountains, alpine meadows, forests, and grasslands

Habits
Most active in early morning and evening, but can adjust if necessary; use strong sense of smell to identify both prey and fellow bears; live alone except when raising cubs

Diet
Will eat just about anything, including grass, roots, berries, insects, ground squirrels, and elk and bison calves

Distinctive Features
Hair on back and shoulders has light, frosted-looking tips; muscular back for digging; large claws for tearing and digging; able to stand on hind legs

Fast Fact
Grizzly mothers are very protective of their young cubs.

Average Size

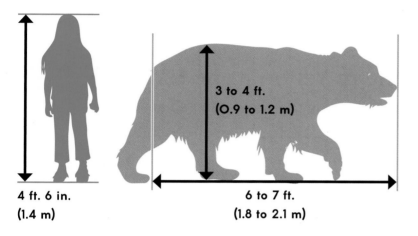

4 ft. 6 in.
(1.4 m)

3 to 4 ft.
(0.9 to 1.2 m)

6 to 7 ft.
(1.8 to 2.1 m)

Human (age 10)

Grizzly Bear

Classification

CLASS
Mammalia
(mammals)

ORDER
Carnivora
(bears, tigers, wolves,
and related animals)

FAMILY
Ursidae
(bears)

GENUS
Ursus
(bears)

SPECIES
Ursus arctos
(brown bears)

SUBSPECIES
Ursus arctos horribilis
(grizzly bears)

◀ Grizzlies have small
ears, but their hearing
is excellent.

CHAPTER 1

Majestic Giants

It's springtime in Yellowstone National Park. The sun shines, melting the snow piled all around. A male grizzly bear awakens. He has been asleep in his den all winter. The bear moves slowly at first. You would, too, if you'd been asleep for five or six months!

The bear lumbers out of his den and blinks into the bright sunshine. He rises on powerful legs—he's over 6 feet (1.8 meters) tall when standing. The bear sniffs the air, then sets off through the sagebrush in search of a meal. He'll munch on grass at first. But it won't be long before his quest for meat begins.

Grizzlies are a type of brown bear. They once roamed across the western half of North America, from up north in the Arctic all the way south to central Mexico. But those days are gone. Today grizzlies are found only in the states of Alaska, Wyoming, Washington, Idaho, and Montana. There are also grizzlies in northern Canada.

▶ Grizzlies' lips aren't attached to their gums, so they're very stretchy.

A Bear's Neighborhood

What do you consider to be your neighborhood? Is it your street? Your part of town? A grizzly bear's idea of a neighborhood, known as its home range, is much bigger.

A male grizzly's home range can be 300 to 500 square miles (777 to 1,295 square kilometers). Female grizzlies have smaller ranges, especially when they are raising cubs. The size of the range probably has to do with the amount of food available in the area, as well as the number of bears competing for that food.

There are usually different habitats within a grizzly's home range. There might be meadows and forests, as well as valleys and mountains. Different habitats mean a variety of food options for bears.

Grizzlies are solitary animals. Bear cubs stay close to their mothers, but adult grizzlies wander their ranges alone. Grizzlies don't mind other bears being in their home range. They aren't very territorial, as long as there's enough to eat!

◀ Grizzlies are called "silvertips" because of the light fur on their backs.

Built for Power

The grizzly bear is one of the largest carnivores in North America. On average, adult male grizzlies weigh 600 pounds (272.2 kilograms). Females are smaller, weighing around 300 lb. (136.1 kg).

You might think animals of that size would be slow, but you'd be wrong. Grizzly bears can run as fast as 35 mi. (56.3 km) per hour over short distances. That's faster than even the fastest Olympic runners. Grizzlies don't race each other, though. They use their speed to chase down prey.

Grizzlies are very powerful diggers, too, often using their claws to find food. They dig in the dirt to catch moles and other rodents that tunnel underground. They pull up tree stumps to eat the roots and the insects living underneath. Grizzlies also use their powerful claws to dig out their winter dens.

Tail is less than 8 in. (20.3 cm) long.

Fast Fact
Unlike cat claws, grizzly claws don't retract—they're always out.

Hump
is made of muscle, and it makes grizzlies very good at digging.

Face
is concave (or "dished out"); other bears have straighter faces.

Fur
on the grizzly's shoulders and back has white tips.

Front Teeth
are sharp for ripping into meat. Back teeth are flat for grinding up food.

Claws
are 2 to 4 in. (5.1 to 10.2 cm) long.

11

Smell Ya Later

Humans have five senses, but most of us depend on our sense of sight the most. Our eyes tell us where we are. They help us understand what's nearby and what's far away. Grizzlies gather that information through their noses instead. In fact, bears may have the best sense of smell of any animal.

All animals have special cells in their noses called smell receptors. The more smell receptors an animal has, the better its ability to smell is. Grizzly noses have about 100 times as many receptors as human noses do.

This means grizzly bears can smell food from miles away—even if the food is underwater! Grizzlies also recognize each other by smell. A grizzly can easily sniff out another grizzly that wanders into its territory. Bears use their noses to understand their world, the way we use our eyes.

It is a myth that grizzlies have bad eyesight. Grizzly eyes work fine—bears just depend more on their sense of smell.

▶ Grizzlies are often drawn to campsites by the smell of humans' food.

Brown, but Not Grizzly

The term "brown bear" is a category that includes a few types of bears. The grizzly is one **subspecies** of brown bear. There are other subspecies, too, like the Kodiak bear and the Syrian bear. Think of it this way: All grizzlies are brown bears, but not all brown bears are grizzlies.

It is pretty common for people to use the word "grizzly" to mean any brown bear at all. Unfortunately, this means learning about grizzlies can be a somewhat confusing experience! For example, you might have seen nature shows on TV where "grizzly bears" catch salmon from rivers. But in fact, those are not true grizzlies; they are simply brown bears.

Zoologists tell us that true grizzly bears live inland; they do not live along coasts, the way some other brown bears do. There are no salmon in the places where true grizzlies live.

True grizzlies are also smaller than other brown bears. Male brown bears can weigh as much as 850 lb. (385.6 kg). The average grizzly doesn't get quite that big.

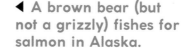

◀ A brown bear (but not a grizzly) fishes for salmon in Alaska.

CHAPTER 2

Surviving the Wild

Grizzlies live in places with long, cold winters. For months, there is very little food available. Bears and other animals use **hibernation** to survive these conditions. Rather than try (and fail) to find food, these animals seek safe, warm spaces to sleep the winter away.

Grizzlies hibernate in dens. Sometimes they find spots that make good natural dens, like rock crevices and hollowed-out trees. They keep an eye out for these spots all summer long. Grizzlies have good memories—if they notice a good denning site during the summer, they can return to that spot in fall when hibernation begins.

If grizzlies don't find a natural den, they will dig little caves for themselves. That big muscle in the bear's hump is very helpful when it's time to dig. It takes from three to seven days for a bear to create its den. Bears don't usually return to dens they have used in previous years.

Fast Fact
During hibernation, a grizzly's heart rate drops about 80%.

▶ A grizzly emerges from its den after hibernation.

The Hunt

Grizzlies need to add a lot of fat to their bodies in spring and summer. That's the only way they'll survive their long winter's sleep.

A grizzly is smallest in spring. Its first meal after hibernation is usually carrion. The rotten meat helps the grizzly gain strength for the next phase of its dietary cycle: the hunt.

A grizzly uses its sense of smell to find elk and moose, and its speed to catch them. However, a grizzly must spend its energy wisely. Hunting a full-grown moose or elk is hard work! And it's risky because the grizzly could get injured. That's why grizzlies hunt only young animals.

If a bear were to run directly into a herd, the animals would scatter—and the hunter would go hungry. The best situation for a grizzly is to find a calf that has wandered away from its herd. The bear can chase the calf and overpower it. The grizzly uses its claws to slash the prey, then carries it into the woods to eat it.

◀ A grizzly feasts on the remains of a bison.

No Picky Eaters

Grizzlies spend the warmer months gaining weight very rapidly. At its hungriest, a grizzly will eat 90 lb. (40.8 kg) of food in one day. That's about 200 hamburgers!

It's tough finding that much food, and there's no time to be picky. That's why grizzlies are true **omnivores**, meaning that they eat anything and everything! In fact, meat makes up only 10 to 20 percent of their diet. Instead, grizzlies feast on berries, flowers, pinecones, and tree bark. They tear up stumps to get at the roots underneath. And if a grizzly finds a squirrel's collection of nuts? The bear will devour the entire stash—and eat the squirrel, too. Grizzlies that live near people will even dig through garbage cans to find food.

Grizzlies in Yellowstone National Park especially love moths. They can eat 40,000 per day!

Fast Fact
Grizzlies eat honey and may even eat the bees that made it!

▶ When grizzlies are very hungry, just about anything they can catch, snatch, or dig up becomes food.

Moth

Moths' bodies contain a lot of fat, providing important calories for bears.

Roots

Grizzlies dig up plants to eat the roots, plus any insects living underneath.

Squirrel

▶ Grizzlies eat rodents such as mice and squirrels.

Berries

▶ Grizzlies feast on soapberries when they ripen in July.

The Language of Bears

Grizzly bears make themselves understood in a number of ways. For example, if a bear encounters another bear and simply sits down, it's that bear's way of telling the other that he doesn't want to fight. Sitting down is a way of showing **deference**.

Other times, bears make a sound called whuffing, which is like a blend of a cough and a bark. The message: *I'm not happy; something is making me uncomfortable.* It is a way of telling other bears to back off.

If whuffing doesn't work, the grizzly might shift its body sideways to make itself look as big as possible. This is another form of warning. The message is: *Don't you see how big I am? You'd better run!*

But if the bear turns to face another grizzly straight on? Look out! That means the bear has decided to hold its ground. Grizzlies don't go looking for **conflict**, but they don't shy from a fight if they feel threatened.

◀ Grizzlies also sometimes growl. Growling can mean the bear is hurt or angry.

Leave a Message at the Tree

Grizzlies are solitary, but they do have to communicate with other bears sometimes. How can they interact across such large ranges? The answer is written on the trees.

When a grizzly rubs its back against a tree, the bear is not scratching an itch. It's leaving its unique scent on the bark. These "rub trees" are like message boards for grizzlies. Male bears let one another know who is in the area. Females let males know they are looking for mates. Even cubs may use rub trees if they get separated from their mothers.

Rub trees help grizzlies learn to recognize one another. Researchers believe this reduces fights between males. If they know each other by smell, grizzlies are less likely to be hostile when they meet.

Bears don't just leave smells on trees, though. They also leave hair, which scientists analyze for DNA. Rub trees are incredibly useful for scientists who study grizzlies.

▶ This bear's scent will stay on the tree long after he's gone.

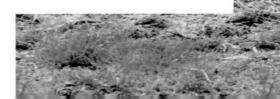

CHAPTER 3

Growing Up Grizzly

It's early summer, and a young male grizzly, called a boar, is following a female, called a sow, through the woods. The boar's keen sense of smell tells him the female is ready to **mate**. But he has to be patient. He trails the sow at a distance for several days.

Before the boar gets a chance to approach the female, though, another male grizzly arrives. Now the young male has to make a decision. Should he fight this bear for the female's attention?

The young boar sniffs the air. He recognizes the newcomer by scent—the other male is larger and more experienced than he. The young male understands this is not a fight he can win. He retreats in search of a different female partner.

▶ Once a sow and boar have paired up, the two bears will stay together for several days.

Welcome, Cubs

Mating season for grizzly bears lasts from May to July. A female grizzly bear can mate with several males during that time. In autumn, she prepares a den and gets ready to hibernate. She will give birth to her cubs during hibernation.

There's a lot we don't know about grizzly births. Researchers have placed tiny cameras in bear dens to try to find out what happens. It seems mother grizzlies do wake up briefly during or right after the birth. Cameras have spotted mothers waking up and licking their cubs before going back to sleep.

Grizzlies can have from one to four cubs at a time. Newborn cubs weigh only about 1 lb. (0.5 kg). The newborn cubs have no fur, and they're born blind. Because grizzlies are **mammals**, their first food is their mother's milk. They begin **nursing** right away, while their mother sleeps. And they grow fast! By springtime, the cubs weigh around 8 lb. (3.6 kg). They are ready to eat solid food, although they also continue to nurse for a while.

◀ These 10-day-old cubs weigh just under 2 lb. (1 kg).

A Cub's Life

Grizzly mothers are famous for being **protective** of their cubs, and with good reason! Female grizzlies have only 10 cubs in their whole lives, and not all will survive. Around 50 to 80 percent of grizzly cubs live into adulthood. Those bears have a good chance of living about 25 years in the wild. Bears in the care of humans can live even longer.

Grizzly cubs stay with their mothers for two to three years. During that time, mothers teach the youngsters everything they know. At first, very young cubs watch their mother **forage** and hunt. Later, the cubs try doing it on their own.

Cubs are very playful. They'll roll down a slope, climb back up, and roll down again. Cubs frequently wrestle with each other. Researchers are not certain why cubs play so much. They may be practicing new skills or burning off extra energy. Or they may just enjoy it!

Eventually, the mother grizzly's body will tell her that it's time to mate again. When this happens, she'll send her cubs away to live on their own.

▶ Cubs play in Denali National Park in Alaska.

CHAPTER 4

The Bear Family

The earliest bears probably looked

like wolves. They got bigger and more bearlike over time.

Prehistoric bears were larger and faster than bears are today. For example, short-faced bears lived in North America more than a million years ago. They were 12 ft. (3.7 m) tall when standing! Thanks to their extra-long legs, these bears could run about 40 miles per hour (64.4 kilometers per hour). Short-faced bears went **extinct** around 10,000 years ago.

More recently, humans have caused several extinctions in the bear family. For example, the California grizzly was a cousin of today's grizzly bears. It roamed the American West as recently as the 1800s. But farmers, ranchers, and gold prospectors considered them dangerous pests. California grizzlies were hunted aggressively and became extinct in the 1920s. The Mexican grizzly met a similar fate in the 1960s.

▶ This is the skeleton of a short-faced bear. It is displayed in a museum in Chicago.

As Close as Cousins

There are eight species of bears, and some are more alike than others. For example, the grizzly's closest relative is the polar bear. You'd never confuse the two, though!

But black bears and brown bears (including grizzlies) can look very similar. Black bears sometimes have brown fur, and brown bears sometimes look black. However, there are ways to tell them apart. Black bears don't have humps like brown bears do. Black bears' faces are straight, rather than dish-shaped. Also, black bears have bigger ears, but smaller claws than brown bears have.

One major difference between black and brown bears is in their behavior. Black bears are very shy—they'd rather hide than fight. A black bear mother may even abandon her cubs to avoid a confrontation. Mama grizzlies, however, won't hesitate to fight if their cubs are in danger.

These behaviors didn't evolve by accident. Black bears live in forests, where they can escape trouble by climbing trees. Brown bears live in open spaces, with fewer places to hide. They have had to be tougher to survive.

◀ Unlike grizzlies, black bears are perfectly comfortable in trees.

CHAPTER 5

Bears and People

Humans and grizzlies shared the land for many years with only occasional conflict. Some Native American tribes hunted them for food and fur. But more often, native people considered bears to be **sacred**. Some tribes believe that the Great Spirit takes the form of the grizzly when on Earth. To them, killing a grizzly would be unthinkable.

The grizzly bear also plays an important role in Native American stories about the origin of the world. The Pawnee tell a story about a young man who is given powers by a grizzly bear. By following the bear's instructions, the man becomes a great warrior. He is also granted healing powers, which is why the story is called "The Grizzly Bear's Medicine."

Today, many native peoples continue to view grizzlies as sacred. This is why they object to grizzly hunting.

▶ In this illustration, a Blackfoot medicine man honors the grizzly with his costume.

Grizzlies Under Pressure

Europeans arrived in North America in large numbers in the 1700s, and they were not interested in sharing the land with grizzlies. These newcomers didn't hold Native American views on the natural world. Europeans viewed nature as something to be tamed.

Grizzlies killed and ate cows that ranchers were working hard to raise. They smashed beehives and chicken coops. And grizzlies could be extremely dangerous, even deadly. To the people who settled the American West, grizzlies were not sacred. They were a problem. Hunters killed as many as they could, as quickly as possible. Within a hundred years, the grizzly population of the continental United States had been reduced by about 90 percent.

Before the West was settled, there were around 50,000 grizzly bears in the lower 48 states. By the 1970s, there were very few left. The U.S. government placed grizzlies on a list of threatened animals. That action made it illegal to hunt them.

◀ Grizzlies are called nuisance bears when they wander too close to human settlements.

Protecting the Umbrella

The effort was successful, and the number of grizzly bears has increased. For example, there were fewer than 200 bears left in Yellowstone National Park in 1975. Today there are about 700. Overall, there are about 30,000 grizzlies in Alaska and about 1,500 in the continental United States.

In 2017, the grizzly was removed from the list of threatened animals. But **conservationists** argued that was too soon to take grizzlies off the list.

It's important to realize that grizzlies interact with a large number of other animals and plants. The bears consume carrion, which limits the spread of disease. They hunt live animals, which prevents overpopulation. They control the spread of certain plants by eating their berries. They keep insect populations low by eating larvae. All this activity helps keep the entire **ecosystem** in balance. That's why the grizzly bear is sometimes described as an umbrella species. When we protect the umbrella, we are protecting the entire ecosystem.

▶ Grizzlies live alongside gray wolves in Yellowstone.

Grizzly Bear Family Tree

Bears are part of the order Carnivora, which includes more than 260 species, such as cats, dogs, wolves, seals, and raccoons. Some animals in this order feed exclusively on meat. Others are omnivorous. They eat meat as well as other foods, such as plants, fruits, and honey. All the animals in this order share a common ancestor that lived about 55 million years ago. This tree shows how grizzlies are related to other members of this order. The closer two animals are on the tree, the more similar they are.

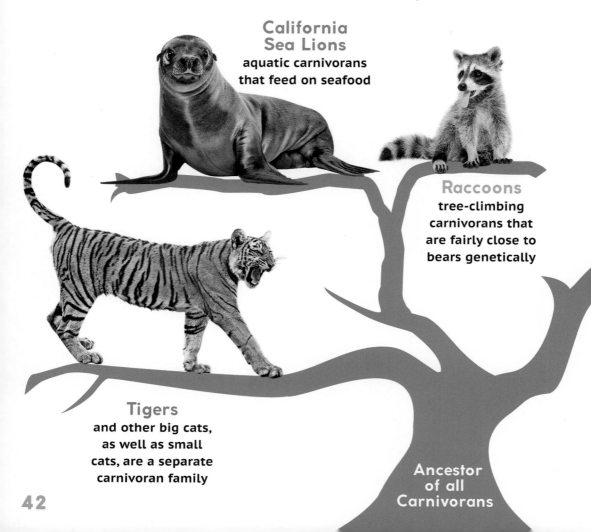

California Sea Lions
aquatic carnivorans that feed on seafood

Raccoons
tree-climbing carnivorans that are fairly close to bears genetically

Tigers
and other big cats, as well as small cats, are a separate carnivoran family

Ancestor of all Carnivorans

Grizzly Bears
brown bears that get as much as 90 percent of their calories from plants

Polar Bears
largest bears in North America

American Black Bears
the smallest type of bear in North America

Note: Animal photos are not to scale.

Words to Know

C .... **carnivores** *(KAHR-nuh-vorz)* animals that eat meat

carrion *(KA-ree-en)* the flesh of dead animals

conflict *(KAHN-flikt)* a serious disagreement

conservationists *(kahn-sur-VAY-shun-ists)* people who protect valuable things, especially forests, wildlife, or natural resources

D .... **deference** *(DEH-frens)* a way of behaving that shows respect for someone or something

den *(DEN)* the home of a wild animal

DNA *(DEE-en-AY)* the molecule that carries our genes, found inside the nucleus of cells

E .... **ecosystem** *(EE-koh-sis-tuhm)* all the living things in a place and their relation to their environment

extinct *(ik-STINGKT)* no longer found alive

F .... **forage** *(FOR-ij)* to go in search of food

H .... **habitats** *(HAB-i-tats)* the places where an animal or plant is usually found

herd *(HURD)* a large group of animals

hibernation *(hye-bur-NAY-shun)* the act of sleeping for the entire winter; this protects animals and helps them survive when the temperatures are cold and food is hard to find

M.......... **mammals** *(MAM-uhlz)* warm-blooded animals that have hair or fur and usually give birth to live babies; female mammals produce milk to feed their young

mate *(MAYT)* to join together for breeding

N .... **nursing** *(NURS-ing)* drinking milk from a breast

O .... **omnivores** *(AHM-nuh-vorz)* animals or people that eat both plants and meat

P .... **prey** *(PRAY)* animals that are hunted by another animal for food

protective *(pruh-TEK-tiv)* having or showing a strong desire to protect someone or something from harm

R .... **receptors** *(re-SEP-turz)* sense organs

rodents *(ROH-duhnts)* mammals with large, sharp front teeth that are constantly growing and used for gnawing things

S .... **sacred** *(SAY-krid)* holy, or having to do with religion

solitary *(SAH-li-ter-ee)* not requiring or without the companionship of others

subspecies *(sub-SPEE-sheez)* a group of related plants or animals that is smaller than a species; a division of a species

T .... **territorial** *(ter-i-TOR-ee-uhl)* defensive of an area against others, especially of the same species

threatened *(THRET-uhnd)* at risk of becoming endangered

Z .... **zoologists** *(zoh-AH-luh-jists)* scientists who study animal life

Find Out More

BOOKS

- Ballard, Jack. *Grizzly Bears*. Guilford, CT: Globe Pequot, 2012.
- Carney, Elizabeth. *Bears (National Geographic Readers Series)*. Washington, D.C.: National Geographic Society, 2016.
- Wilkinson, Todd. *Grizzly: The Bears of Greater Yellowstone*. New York: Rizzoli, 2015.

WEB PAGES

- defenders.org/grizzly-bear/basic-facts

  Information about grizzlies from Defenders of Wildlife, a conservationist organization.

- www.nationalgeographic.com/animals/mammals/g/grizzly-bear

  Information, photos, and videos about grizzlies from National Geographic.

- www.nps.gov/yell/learn/nature/grizzlybear.htm

  Lots of information about the grizzlies of Yellowstone National Park, provided by the U.S. National Park Service.

Facts for Now

Visit this Scholastic Web site for more information on grizzly bears: **www.factsfornow.scholastic.com** Enter the keywords *Grizzly Bears*

Index

Index *(continued)*

About the Author

H.W. Poole is a writer and editor of books for young people. She's never seen a grizzly bear, but after researching this book she knows just how to tell the difference between a grizzly bear and a brown bear!